I0819003

ISBN: 978-0-578-92979-8

Published by The Coaching Factory www.TheCoachingFactoryLA.com
Contact: Connect@TheCoachingFactoryLA.com
Distributed By: Itasca Books Distribution & Fulfillment www.itascabooks.com
Cover Illustrated By: Reyna Noriega www.ReynaNoriega.com
Graphic Design: Jacob Reel www.JacobReel.com
Graphic Design: Adriane Leigh www.TaruRituals.com
Editor (Executive Coach)**:** Diane Knoepke, Paperweight Advising
Editor (Licensed Mental Health Practitioner)**:** Dr. Jarryn Robinson-Ellis
Editor (Copy)**:** Stephanie Wetzel

The Coaching Factory Team:
Stately Jukes, General Manager
Jacob Reel, Executive Assistant to the CEO

Special Thanks To My Partner: Dr. Marissa A. West

Land Acknowledgement: This book was written on the unceded and traditional territory of the Chumash, Tongva and Fernandeño. I recognize the harrowing history of colonization and pledge to continuously commit myself to lifelong learning and the conscious dismantling of harmful systems.

Disclaimer: Every effort has been made to ensure that this work is helpful to my readers at publishing time. However, this is not a comprehensive guide for all endeavors. No liability is assumed for losses or damages incurred due to the application of information provided.

deepen your connection with *your team*

our very first team

DATE ____________

Our understanding of the word team is defined by our very first teammates, our family.

I invite you to consider your experiences ages 0-16. Family is defined by you.

If you could capture your family experiences in a movie, what would the title be?

DATE ____________

When we begin to think about this period in our lives, all kinds of emotions can surface. Helplessness, shame, anger, confusion, irritation, indifference, gratitude, joy, contentment, pride, fondness, and happiness are common.

What warnings would you want to give to someone else before they watch this film?

1. ____________________

____

2. ____________________

____

3. ____________________

____

The diversity in emotional responses is a result of unique familial experiences and their long term impact on our understanding of self and others. If you noticed strong emotion here, I encourage you to also care for yourself by finding ways to process in relationship (e.g. therapy).

DATE ______________

What was your role on the family team?

Do you see any similarities between your role on that team and the role you play at work now?

DATE ____________

Who was your favorite person on the family team and why?

What does someone have to do to become your favorite now?

Who is someone in your life who may benefit from more attention from you?

DATE ___________

Our brains are 90% developed by the time we're 5 years old[1]. How we're affirmed, supported, disciplined, and loved impacts much of our experience and expectations as an adult.

How was **job well done** communicated in your household, if at all?

____

____

What was one unspoken rule in your family?

____

____

How do the answers above impact what you expect in the workplace? Our implicit rules and limits influence our understanding of ourselves and dictate the types of relationships we foster.

____

____

[1]Ann & Robert H. Lurie Children's Hospital of Chicago

DATE ____________

What is something you learned from your first team (your family) that you look for in all other teams?

DATE ____________

What are you carrying from your first team (your family) that may be hindering progress on your current team?

DATE ____________

What superpower are you bringing from your first team (your family) that is helping your current team every day?

DATE ____________

**Our fears, insecurities, and hesitancies were formed long before we stepped foot into a workplace.
They need to be held gently and examined.**

What is one behavior you learned before the age of 16 that may be making teamwork more challenging for you?

DATE ______________

Influential leaders are incredibly self-aware. It's important to understand the reality of who we really are at work.

When we've identified our areas of opportunity, our job is not to "fix" ourselves. We are not machines. Our job is to be aware, do our best to improve in each area, and surround ourselves with teammates who excel at collaboration and other job-related skills.

On your worst day at work, what are three traits that describe you?

A trait = A quality others may experience (e.g. impatient) or that is experienced internally (e.g. self-loathing)

Worst day at work = You're navigating something terribly difficult or you just feel low

1. ______________

2. ______________

3. ______________

DATE ____________

On your best day at work, what are three traits that describe you?

A trait = A quality others may experience (e.g. encouraging) or that is experienced internally (e.g. resilient)

Best day at work = Extraordinary things are happening or you just feel good!

1. ____________
2. ____________
3. ____________

DATE ____________

Culture develops whether we manage it or not, so let's intentionally develop the culture we want.

Culture = *Core Values* + *Norms*

What's important to us — *What we do repeatedly*

Alignment

Core Value = Diversity	**Norm** = Board reflects many ages, lived experiences, etc.
Core Value = Communication	**Norm** = 100% respond to emails by the deadline
Core Value = Ethical Standards	**Norm** = Recuse ourselves when necessary
Core Value = Work Ethic	**Norm** = Task force work is robust, not driven by one

Misalignment

Core Value = Healthy living	**Norm** = I exercise once a year
Core Value = Innovation	**Norm** = I shut down new ideas
Core Value = Inclusivity	**Norm** = I sit with the same crew every meeting
Core Value = Agility	**Norm** = I've done x the same way for 20 years

What are 3 ways your core values + norms are aligned?

1. ____________
2. ____________
3. ____________

What are 3 ways they're experiencing misalignment?

1. ____________
2. ____________
3. ____________

Feel free to respond based on the culture in your home or your workplace!

high performers are storytellers

DATE ____________

Thinking about our careers can be exhausting. It's not always easy to pick out the stories in our lives that are most impactful for listeners. Use the SCORE framework below to identify moments in your career that are spectacular story engines. For each of the stories you think of below, write a headline that helps you easily bring that story to mind. We'll need this for our next exercise.

Sacrifice | Headline:

Tell a story about a time when you made a significant sacrifice

Choice | Headline:

Tell a story about a time when you made a difficult choice

DATE ______________

Obstacle | Headline:

Tell a story about a time when you overcame a huge obstacle

____

____

____

Risk | Headline:

Tell a story about a time when you took a big risk

____

____

____

Experience | Headline:

Tell a story about a special or unique experience

____

____

____

DATE ______________

Now that you've got your specific stories in mind, let's sharpen our storytelling skills! Pick one story that stands out from the SCORE story engines on the previous pages. Use the four supercharge prompts below to make the story unforgettable!

Human	Set the scene. What was typical or expected about the moment prior to the action? What were you or others doing before things changed? Paint us a picture of the status quo.
Hard	Tell us about a BIG problem, a BIG roadblock, a REAL issue. Tell us about what disrupted the normality you were experiencing.
Heroic	What did you or someone else do to save the day?
Hope	Wrap it in a bow. Tell us a takeaway that lifts and inspires.

DATE ____________

DATE ____________

**High performers who can't tell their own stories get lumped into the same category as low performers.
Learn to tell your story to anyone, anywhere.**

When is the next time you'll get to practice storytelling? Think of both opportunities and obligations.

DATE ______________

In high-performing teams, when one of us wins, we all win.

When one of us makes it into a room, we ALL make it into the room.

Whose story can you learn more deeply and in more detail, so you can be a stronger advocate for them when you get into the room? What do you need to know about them to tell their story with passion?

DATE ____________

The rooms we're winning in for ourselves and others are not just physical rooms—they're virtual too! We can stand out and make incredible impressions anywhere, through a screen or in real life. Working virtually is only an obstacle if you decide it is an obstacle.

If you are a person who understands their own power, you are powerful in an office, a grocery store, an after-school pick up line, or at a kitchen counter.

Our power surges through us, shaped by all of our experiences and only stops if we think it stops. Here are ways to shine—even virtually!

- Camera always on
  (If you need to step away or turn your camera off, say so in the chat and continue to actively participate as much as you can)
- First to arrive
- Know ALL materials front and back
- Be prepared to lead with an intentional relationship builder (e.g., an exercise, a question, a kick-off topic, etc.). If you have a small team, here's an idea on the next page.

DATE ______________

Take a look at the example below for a low-lift, high-impact example:

Super Quick Team Hello

The 3 H's

Something making you HAPPY
Something that is HARD
Something bringing you HEALING

Meghan
Jacob
Chelsea
Stately

Pro Tips:

1. Adding the names to the screen eliminates the guesswork of who's next, makes a smooth meeting, and shows the team you're not afraid to put in work ahead of time.
2. Add your planned activity to the agenda or meeting invitation and share in advance to serve those who do not find it easy to gather and share thoughts in real time.

DATE ______________

The times before and after meetings are WIDE OPEN SLAM DUNK OPPORTUNITIES to support your work and team members while demonstrating your power and value.

Some examples:

- Email or message the team: “Here’s a task list and accompanying deadlines for the squad based on our convo.”
- Share a summary of the book mentioned in a meeting, as a follow-up or to prep for an upcoming conversation
- Follow up with a team member on an upcoming trip they are excited about: “You noted you’re headed to Amalfi for the first time. Here is a link to our favorite hotel, Il San Pietro, and recommendations for three restaurants that all show availability during your trip! Can’t wait to hear about your adventure!”

psychological safety and belonging

DATE ____________

Employees who have toxic managers are 60% more likely to suffer a heart attack.[2] The work we do on psychological safety is literally life-saving.

Psychological Safety is experienced when all people on a team share new ideas, mistakes, and feedback without risk of professional, mental, or relational harm.[3]

Who is the leader that has created the most psychologically safe environment for you?

[2]Journal of Occupational & Environmental Medicine Managerial Leadership 2009

[3]The Coaching Factory

DATE ______________

Psychological safety does not automatically exist. It must be offered and received via actions. The offerer does not get to declare the presence of psychological safety—only the receiver can do that. What makes one person feel safe and secure may make another person feel unsafe and anxious. The only remedy here is to share about ourselves, learn about our people, and demonstrate we care deeply.

What is one action someone at work has taken that caused you to feel **psychologically safe**?

What is one action someone at work has taken that caused you to feel **anxious**?

DATE ______________

Let's talk about Diversity, Inclusion, Equity, and Belonging. Psychological safety depends on being able to bring and use our identities, cultures, and experiences with us in each moment.

	Defined By	Summary	How to Assess	Translation	Illustration
Diversity Hands Engaged	The Presence of Difference	Numbers	People Metrics	"Come!"	"Everyone come to our pie competition."
Inclusion Minds Engaged	When All Are Leveraged	Attitudes	Experiences	"Come and actually help!"	"Please bake a pie of your choice and present your creation to the judges."
Equity Pockets Engaged	Equal Access to Winning	Barriers Removed	Processes, Policies, and Their Application	"Come and help, and here is everything you need to have what I have!"	"Here is how your pie will be critiqued, here is $100 rideshare credit for grocery store transportation, biographies on each judge, and a 20-minute consultation with a private pastry chef to brainstorm on your idea."
Belonging Hearts Engaged	When All Are Celebrated	Stories	Surveys and Polling	"You self-identify as one of us and we honor your individual story, too! Lead us in how our team can work to attract/retain more talent like you."	"Your outstanding vegan apple pie won the competition. Thank you for leading us in thinking through what participants will need next year to participate in the best pie competition ever!"

In your current organization, what's needed to ensure everyone has equal access to winning?

DATE ____________

Race is one of the ways we perceive and experience difference within our teams. Yet race is not a biological construct or scientific truth. The story of race was invented by humans to justify the enslavement of humans and genocide of Indigenous people.[4]

When did you first become aware of race?

Share a memory from childhood that shaped who you view as a safe place, obstacle, or enemy in this world.

[4] University of California, Berkeley

DATE ____________

One barrier to equity is unacknowledged privilege.

Privilege: A privilege is a right, favor, advantage, or immunity specially granted to one individual or group and withheld from another.[5]

We all experience privilege in some way every single day and we use that privilege to make our lives better.

I am a Black, Chinese, Jamaican, Queer woman and I strive to live a life guided by Jesus*. These are five ways I experience privilege every day:

- English is My First Language
- Parents are Homeowners
- U.S. Passport Holder
- Access to Capital
- Access to Legal Counsel

What is the most profound way you experience privilege on a day-to-day basis?

---

[5]Merriam-Webster Dictionary

*My faith in God is the foundation of my relationship with purpose, dreaming, and achieving. I recognize the harm that many have experienced from religious organizations and people throughout time who have used their power to abuse and oppress others. I invite you to personalize references to God in a way that feels meaningful to you—whether as love, justice, friend, or source.

DATE ____________

**Many of the ways we experience privilege are totally out of our control and are circumstances we're born into. The ask is not that we walk around everywhere apologizing.
(Although there are certainly appropriate times for that).**

The ask is that we do everything humanly possible to acknowledge the fact that we are experiencing an irrefutable, game-changing advantage that someone else is not, and <u>we are not ok with that</u>.

**This is called being actively aware of our privilege.
Actively aware means we live a life constantly prepared to *do something*. In each setting we find ourselves in, we must ask ourselves the following questions:**

1. How am I experiencing privilege right now?
2. What can I do to center those who are not experiencing privilege in this setting?

"You can't get the beautiful 'R' words, like **redemption** and **reconciliation** and **restoration** and **repair**, unless you first tell the truth."

-Bryan Stevenson

Human Rights Lawyer, Author, Founder of Equal Justice Initiative

DATE ____________

Now that we've identified ways we experience privilege, let's talk about allyship.

Allyship:
I will stand **next to you** to ensure you're treated justly.

Abolitionism:
I will **risk something** that is important to me to ensure you're treated justly.[6]

Both of these are important because they shift atmospheres, teams, and cultures. I want to challenge you today to think about abolitionism.

What are you prepared to risk today so someone else is treated justly?

[6]The Coaching Factory

DATE ____________

Thinking of how you show up in your work or community team around issues of equity, circle where you are today on the allyship continuum below.

Allyship Continuum: A range of behaviors or expressions that one can do in demonstration of allyship as developed by Griffin and Haro 2006:

1. Actively participating in harm/oppression
2. Denying/Ignoring
3. Recognizing, No Action
4. Recognizing, Action
5. Educating Self
6. Educating Others
7. Supporting/Encouraging
8. Initiating/Preventing

What do you think is the key for you to get to the next number?

DATE ____________

We all think certain things about certain groups. This does not = bad person, this = **human**.

Racism & Oppression Appear When We	Sounds Like
Think we are neutral about a certain group	"I treat everyone the same. I love ________ people."
Have not examined why we think what we think	"I'm good. Therapy is for people who have been abused."
Allow what we think to influence how we treat others	"If they hadn't dressed like that in here, I would have been happy to help them."

John Rice, a Yale trustee and CEO of Management Leadership for Tomorrow, makes our call to action clear:

> *"We have to increase the cost of racist behavior."*

Think of a time when someone challenged racist behavior—what about their actions inspired you most?

DATE ______________

Let's look at a less-acknowledged factor and area of uneven privilege: domestic overload.

Domestic overload occurs when conditions in an individual's family life, outside of their control, affect their performance at work and/or their appetite for risk-taking.
Let's look at an example:

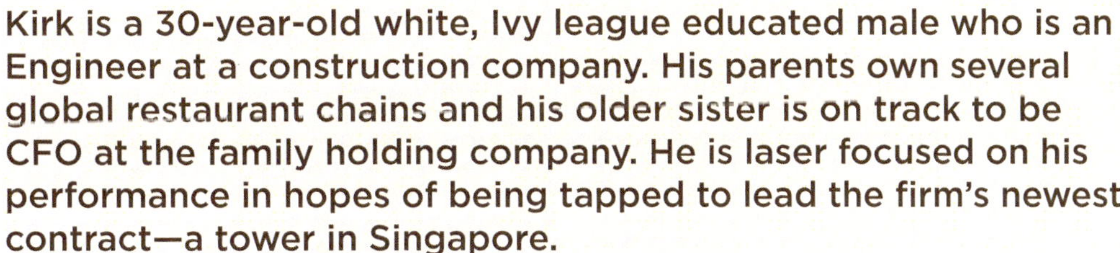

Kirk is a 30-year-old white, Ivy league educated male who is an Engineer at a construction company. His parents own several global restaurant chains and his older sister is on track to be CFO at the family holding company. He is laser focused on his performance in hopes of being tapped to lead the firm's newest contract—a tower in Singapore.

Clara is a 30-year-old Cuban, Ivy league educated woman who is an Engineer at a construction company. Clara has 2 younger brothers. She was raised by a single Father who was injured on the job as a delivery driver. He is on disability indefinitely. She loves her job but is laser focused on each paycheck so she can send 50% home to her family.

Kirk is much more likely to reach the top of this ecosystem, and in record time.

DATE ______________

This example reminds us that talent is everywhere, but opportunities vary greatly as a result of centuries of oppression and current levels of privilege.

What comes up for you as you reflect on the story of Kirk and Clara?

DATE ____________

Oliver is a 19-year-old Venezuelan from Pacoima, CA. Let's spend some time learning about his story.

10 Days with Oliver	Data	
Oliver is a first generation college student and he's excited!	California is home to almost 11 million immigrants. Half of CA children have at least one immigrant parent.	PUBLIC POLICY INSTITUTE OF CA
On his first day, a classmate makes a joke about his parents smuggling him into the U.S. (Oliver and his parents are documented residents). This is nothing he hasn't heard before. He shakes it off.	More than 52% of California's immigrants are naturalized US citizens, and another 25% have another legal status. Only about 23% of immigrants in California are undocumented.	CENTER FOR MIGRATION STUDIES
Oliver is in school part time and works at a music store and Trader Joe's to keep the family afloat. He also cares for his younger sister.	Nationally, white families are wealthier than all other racial groups combined.	CA BUDGET & POLICY CENTER
School is going well, and Oliver is excelling. But Oliver's mom contracts COVID-19. She can no longer work at the grocery story and Oliver is mentally scattered and scared.	Pacoima, CA had one of the highest COVID-19 rates in the country. 1 in 5 residents were infected as opposed to 1 in 24 residents in Brentwood, CA.	LA COUNTY DEPT OF PUBLIC HEALTH
Oliver picks up more hours at Trader Joe's. He is now going to school and working 35 hours a week.	Latinx people: • Are less likely to be able to work from home • Hesitate to engage with the healthcare system due to language barriers or past discriminatory experiences • Are more likely to live in multigenerational housing where social distancing is challenging • Have a higher rate of pre-existing conditions and less access to care	CENTER FOR DISEASE CONTROL
Oliver was helping his 7-year-old sister get dressed and remembered he needed help with an online form. Oliver called his community college for help with only 14 minutes left until the deadline. The person who answered chastised him for waiting.so.long.		

What comes up for you as you reflect on Oliver's story?

DATE ____________

I've heard some companies say phrases like, "We need unconscious bias training." This statement always intrigues me. Primarily because as Melissa Donaldson (The first Chief Diversity Officer at Wintrust Financial) reminds us, not all bias is unconscious.

As we try to get to the root of attitudes and behaviors that keep us from meeting our potential as a team, it can be more helpful to ask these questions:

- What is the real problem we are trying to solve?
- What resources are we ready to spend to solve it?
- Who do we have in place who has a lived experience that aligns with what we're aiming to learn and improve within our team? What is the best way to invite them to inform or lead this work?
- What additional incentive and compensation is ready to be deployed for this extra work?
- What data is our story telling?
- Is this a story that we are proud of?

Which data point at work needs to shift to increase your sense of pride?

DATE ____________

What will you commit to doing today?

Internal Action Pledge

External Action Pledge

Reading
Listening
Asking Questions
Deciding

Sponsorship
Encourage 2 Teammates Today
Working Polls
Active Awareness of Privilege

External Action Pledge Commitment:

____

DATE ____________

Where there are humans, we have conflict. Conflict can be healthy and generative, or it can be heated and toxic. Conflict de-escalation techniques do not teach us how to make conflict go away. Conflict de-escalation techniques teach us how to reduce the intensity of the conflict.

Who is the best conflict de-escalator you know and what do you admire about them?

Thank them for their inspiration today if you can! If they're an ancestor, do something they would have loved.

DATE ____________

Many conflicts arise because someone is feeling fear.

Much of our job as leaders is managing fear.
This is difficult because at work, people don't often say, "I'm afraid!" It's more likely you'll hear something like:

"I just got the deck like 30 seconds ago, but here goes nothing."

Translates to: I'm afraid you might think I am dropping the ball, but I want to prove it's not my fault!

"The color here is probably awful, but this is a start."

Translates to: I'm afraid what I did isn't good enough.

When is the last time you found yourself managing fear?

DATE ____________

We can't talk about psychological safety without talking about fear. When you experience fear at work, which animal below most closely resembles your response?

Eagle	I feel it. Face it. Talk about it. Overcome it. I declare I'm an overcomer!
Spider	I reach out to close friends and ask if my fear is rational. I weave a web of information then re-emerge and proceed based on feedback.
Cheetah	I run away. Fast. I may eventually return to address my fears but my initial reaction is flight.
Hippo	I sit and wait until the fear disappears. It always does.

Is there another animal that isn't listed that resembles your response to fear?

____

No right or wrong animal! The better you understand the type of animal you are, the more successful you'll be at work. The more you understand the animal that is most applicable to your team members, the better teammate you will be.

DATE ____________

Fear has LOYAL friends:

- Unwarranted competitiveness
- Lack of boundaries
- Paranoia
- Health challenges
- Stress

There are many ways people try to remove fear, and some are more fruitful than others. For instance:

Fruitful

- Books
- Therapy
- Journaling

Unfruitful

- Avoiding
- Being mad at themselves for being afraid
- Being mad at others for being afraid

The fastest way fear disappears:

- Encouragement from another human

When you feel fear, what is one healthy behavior you want to engage in?

DATE ______________

What are you feeling afraid of in this season of your life?

What healthy actions help you self soothe?

-
-

DATE ____________

The Psychological Safety Formula

	Definition	Examples of Application
S	Start with the understanding that we know nothing. There is always something we don't know	• "How's your Grandpa, Raj?" • "Anything else you think I should be thinking about to solve this?"
A	Allow people to choose their own adventure & provide consent	• "Would you like me to attend?" • "What does support from me look like?" • "Let's co-create this together." • "Let me know what time is best for you." • "Part of my process is..."
F	Focus on listening. Do not attempt to multitask	• Listen 3x more than I speak • Stop to help in the midst of chaos
E	Expect to learn about topics that are not intrinsic to you	• Rosh Hashanah • Diwali • Neurodivergence
T	Talk about your mistakes	• "I should've looped you in on that! I'm sorry." • "I did the exact same thing!"
Y	Yes, and new ideas	• "Yes, and that will mean we need 2 more weeks!"

DATE ____________

Communicate Inclusively

If our goal is to be someone that can connect with anyone, we have to practice.

It will take a lot of trial and error, but the result is worth it! We practice using "I statements." We also avoid generalizing, expecting the labels in our minds to automatically be appropriate for others, and asking one person to speak on behalf of huge groups. Here are some ways to practice below:

Inflammatory/I Don't Want To Connect	I Respect You & I Want To Connect
All these young people never...	In my experience, I've noticed ________. What's your experience?
Hey guys!	Hey team!
What do you do?	What's bringing you joy right now?
We need more minorities	We need more ___________ to reflect the communities we serve
They suffer from cerebral palsy	They live with cerebral palsy
That's a handicap space	That's an accessible parking space
Do you have a wife?	Do you have a partner?
Jordan is wheelchair-bound	Jordan lives his life in a wheelchair
Can you tell the group what people like you think?	I recognize that the responsibility to learn lies with me. I apologize if this comes as an added burden. Whenever your schedule permits can you tell me more about...
Never OK = Kiddo, Gal, Squirt, Old Man, Beautiful, Sweetheart	Provided & Approved Names

We don't need to be perfect, we just need to TRY.

DATE ______________

One way I can strengthen my communication is by:

____

real teammates give real instructions

DATE ____________

If someone is watching a child we love, we provide specific instructions.

- No nuts
- One hour of screen time max

If someone is watching a pet we love, we provide specific instructions.

- No wet food
- To be walked 3x a day, especially at noon

If there is a family heirloom we want to protect, we provide extremely specific instructions.

- Orange key ring, unlock gray file cabinet, code 5531, open box labeled wolverine

The more important something is to us, the more specific our instructions.

For some reason, in the workplace, we just HOP IN and very rarely provide instructions on how to make us feel safe, how to get the best work product out of us, when to connect with us, via what medium, and what to do if we sense misalignment. If we want to keep ourselves safe, we should be prepared to share specific instructions regarding our needs.

DATE ______________

What are 7 instructions that would accompany YOU to work?

Be specific. For instance, here are my 7:

1. Time and respect are inextricably tied for me. Please be on time to meetings we set. If you aren't able to make it, just let me know asap and I'm thankful!
2. If you need to reach me quickly, send me a text letting me know, and I'll call you via phone from a quiet place.
3. Please share feedback with me directly.
4. I LOVE music—especially loud music—but I cannot actually work with it playing. So we gotta pick lol: music or work. :)
5. I have sound sensitivity. Repeated unnecessary noises like the clicking of a pen make me extremely anxious.
6. I don't eat cow or pig, but I love chicken, seafood, smoothies, and dessert!
7. Please do not call me "girl" in any setting, for any reason.

1. ______________________________
2. ______________________________
3. ______________________________
4. ______________________________
5. ______________________________
6. ______________________________
7. ______________________________

DATE ____________

The most influential leaders know a lot about practices, traditions, and values that do not pertain to their own lives.

What is one culture you will learn more about this week?

DATE ______________

We can't demand change from others; we have to inspire it.

What is one action you can take today to inspire your team?

Hint: People are inspired by acts of humanity. They don't have to be deep; they just need to be real. Here are some examples:

- Logging off early to care for yourself—and naming it
- Going the extra mile to save someone else time on a project
- Coming up with a creative solution to a problem that everyone else forgot about
- Remembering a teammate's mom's birthday party and asking how it went

Would love to hear what you did! #PracticeMakesPeaceful!

DATE ____________

Performance looks different to every stakeholder. Be sure you know what a WIN looks like for your boss, your significant other, and your peers.

What is one relationship—that you're currently in—where you are unclear on how that person defines a win?

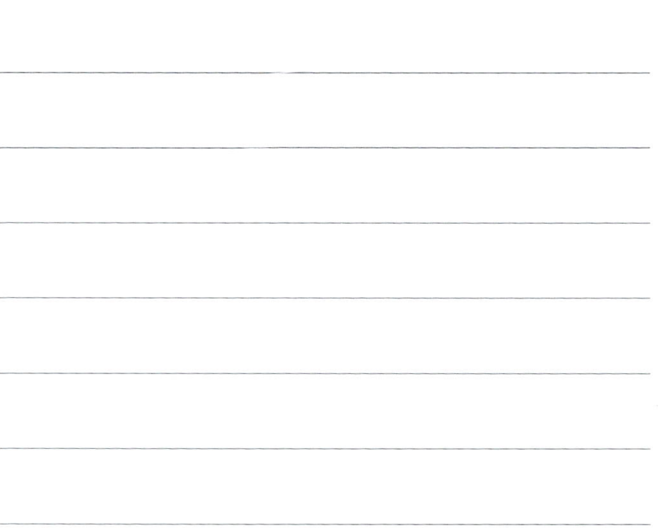

DATE ___________

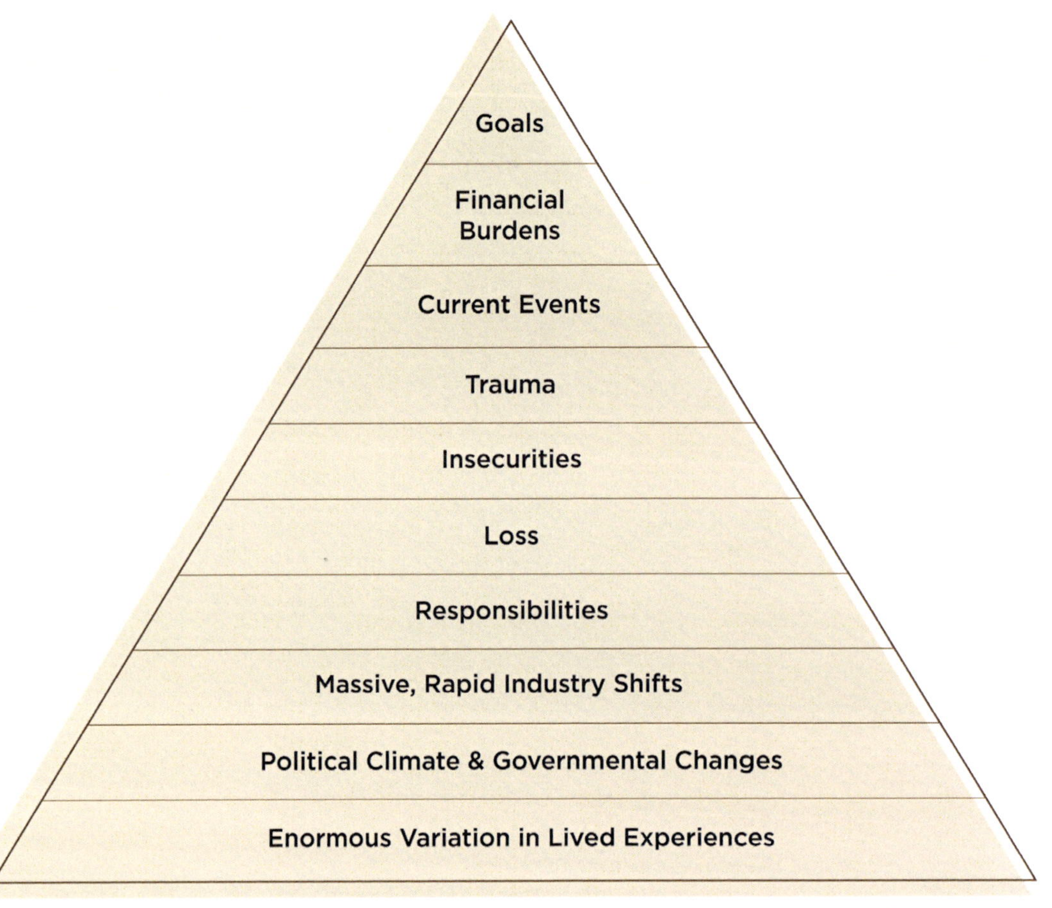

Work is hard. Working in teams is hard. Leading teams is hard! All of us are carrying these massive pyramids above, then we're placed with OTHER people and THEIR pyramids, and we're expected to "GO MAKE A HIGH-PERFORMANCE TEAM!"

This is what happens every day at work. That is the ask.

DATE ____________

Which section of your pyramid feels heaviest right now?

What practices are you currently engaging in that bring **relief** from that weight?

DATE ______________

Feedback is information communicated to another person or group that explains <u>your point of view</u> on their work, style, decisions, and actions. The goal of feedback should be to inspire behavior that will take the listener to higher heights.

Before you give someone feedback, it may be helpful to ask yourself, "Is this a business problem or a personal preference?"

- **Business problem=** Behavior is impacting money or performance.
- **Personal Preference=** Behavior is different from what I or another colleague would do.

Encourage. Encourage. Encourage. Then, step in when a business problem presents.

Critical feedback should be used as a tool, not a weapon.

The difference between feedback and coaching is the level of trust required.

Be very thoughtful when providing feedback. Take the time to get all of your thoughts together. Excellent talent will leave you if you piss them off, and I don't blame them one bit.

DATE ____________

58% of people trust total strangers more than their own boss.[7]

Trust is easily broken at work when leaders have not practiced providing timely, fair, focused feedback (i.e. given refined instructions). Giving excellent feedback takes practice.

Each person has different needs, and it takes some trial and error. Here's where to start:

Feedback: The Art of Delivery

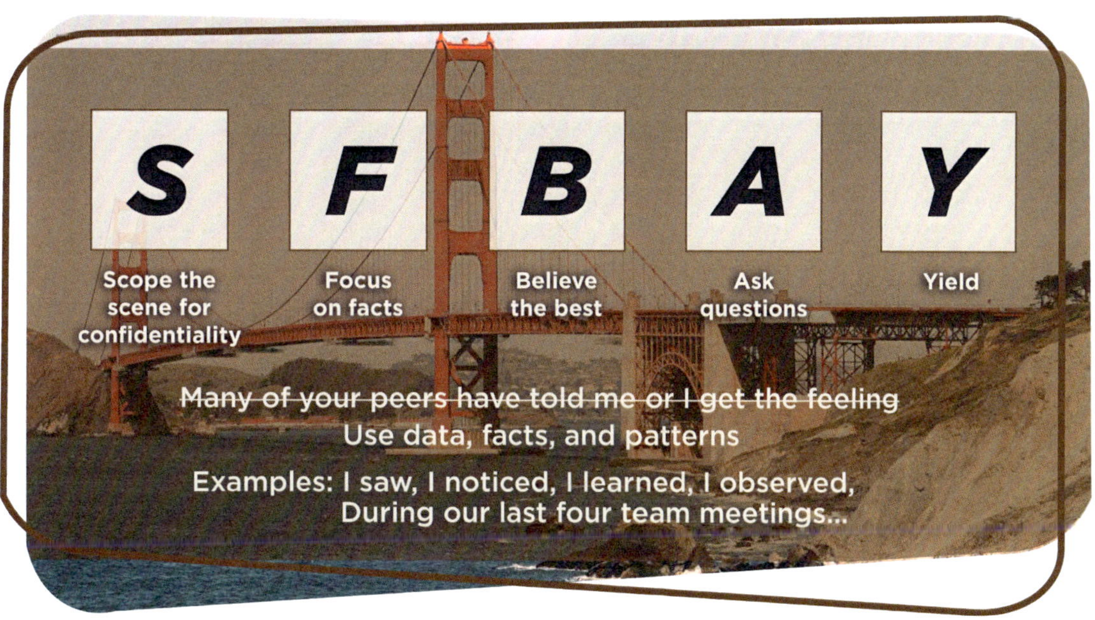

[7]Harvard Business Review

Pro Tip:

The most fruitful working relationships have systems in place that allow everyone to receive feedback, not just some people at some levels. Here's what has worked best for our team.

Lisa is Michelle's manager. Each Thursday at 1PM, during their 1:1 they both take time to reflect and share feedback.

Michelle self-reflects with Lisa:

- Where she believes she really shined this week
- What she would like to think more about or continue to sharpen

Lisa shares with Michelle:

- Where she believes Michelle really shined this week
- What Michelle may want to think more about or continue to sharpen

THEN (This is the fun part: reverse feedback)

Lisa self-reflects with Michelle:

- Where she believes she really shined this week
- What she would like to think more about or continue to sharpen

Michelle shares with Lisa:

- Where Michelle believes Lisa really shined this week
- What Lisa may want to think more about or sharpen

DATE ____________

This is a special practice because it provides a structured opportunity for people to practice giving feedback, accepting feedback, strategizing for conversations, identifying their own gaps, and building trust at any level.

Depending on the size of your team and business rhythms, this exact model may or may not be feasible, but a regular rhythm where everyone receives celebration and feedback is a game changer.

Bonus: If you're working hard to adjust one specific behavior, set a DISASTER PLAN.

Disaster Plan= What the person should do if the original plan isn't working or panic sets in!

Sounds Like This: "If you aren't able to gather the data by tomorrow at 4PM ET, please send me a message on Teams, and we'll navigate next steps together."

Is there anyone in your sphere who would benefit from making a disaster plan with you today?

DATE ____________

Read the room, but don't forget you're a writer in there too!

- A quick way to lose a room is to give valid feedback at the wrong time
- Know where you are in the process
- Staying calm is a superpower
- Is it time to:
  - Share your knowledge? (No need to "piggyback")
  - Push for an idea?
  - Raise a concern that may happen as a result of an idea?
  - Recenter a conversation?
  - Be quiet?
  - Ask a question?
  - Shine a light on someone else who deserves it?
- Take your time practicing your discernment #PracticeMakesPeaceful

What trusted advisors or mechanisms do you have in place to help you gauge how effectively you're showing up?

DATE ____________

Executive presence is often weaponized against certain people, and that weaponization is common in environments where it goes undefined and undiscussed. So let's talk about Executive Presence.

Before we can begin to sharpen this skill, we must QUIET THE NOISE.

- "I don't want to be too bold"
- "I don't want to do too much"
- "I don't want them to think I'm an overachiever"
- "They're gonna change my responsibilities!"
- "Everything is shifting, and I don't know what's gonna happen with my role"
- "They are already so tight, and I am new to this team"
- "I SHOULD be further along by now"
- "I work remotely so I'll never get more visibility"

The Coaching Factory's Executive Presence Spectrum™

DISENGAGED/ AVOIDANT PRESENCE

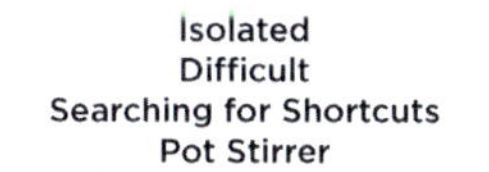

Isolated
Difficult
Searching for Shortcuts
Pot Stirrer
Focused on the Wrong Outcomes
Complainer

LEARNING/EMERGING PRESENCE

Absorbing
Watching
Applying
Noting Missteps
Working
Growing
Connecting

LEADING/SOLVING PRESENCE

Vessel for Answers
Thought Leader
Effective
Unwavering
Excited & Ignited
Polished
Actively Nurtured by Company Leadership

UNDENIABLE EXECUTIVE PRESENCE

Loyal
Room Changer
Kind & Incredibly Thoughtful
Natural Refuge
Decisive
Relentless yet Rational
Relationship Capital Overflows

DATE ____________

Executive Presence Spectrum™ Tool

Please rate yourself on a scale of 1-5

1=Never 2=Once 3=Sometimes 4=Frequently 5=Always

Proven

I intentionally strive to identify my own gaps and grow in those areas ______

I provide specific proposals/plans as opposed to possibilities ______

I consistently devote time to studying my industry by reading news, books, articles etc. ______

I think clearly and express myself well under pressure ______

I am very knowledgeable regarding my work, and I always know more than I say ______

When conflict arises, I take an active (not passive) approach towards a resolution ______

Trustworthy

My non-verbal cues match my words ______

When I'm busy, I still give my best to people ______

I'm quick to give praise to others ______

I don't hesitate to accept responsibility for failure ______

I recognize there are limits to my own knowledge, and I'm comfortable diving into domains outside of my areas of expertise ______

Influential

Colleagues wait for me to start meetings or certainly know when I'm arriving ______

Colleagues stop during meetings to ask my opinion ______

I am rarely interrupted or spoken over ______

DATE ____________

I am comfortable with silence, and I intentionally use silence as a tool ______

I spend time thinking about how I can support my teammates better ______

Polished

People ask my advice on attire and/or soft skills ______

Colleagues at all levels ask me for help handling delicate situations ______

I take every interaction seriously and spend time ensuring I look sharp each day ______

I believe the foundation of my knowledge is sufficient & I'm unafraid to walk into any room to share it ______

Total: _____ ÷20 = ______

1-2

DISENGAGED/ AVOIDANT PRESENCE

Isolated
Difficult
Searching for Shortcuts
Pot Stirrer
Focused on the Wrong Outcomes
Complainer

2-3

LEARNING/EMERGING PRESENCE

Absorbing
Watching
Applying
Noting Missteps
Working
Growing
Connecting

3-4

LEADING/SOLVING PRESENCE

Vessel for Answers
Thought Leader
Effective
Unwavering
Excited & Ignited
Polished
Actively Nurtured by Company Leadership

4-5

UNDENIABLE EXECUTIVE PRESENCE

Loyal
Room Changer
Kind & Incredibly Thoughtful
Natural Refuge
Decisive
Relentless yet Rational
Relationship Capital Overflows

DATE ______________

It is rare for talent to get past the center line unless they have done significant inner work

DISENGAGED/ AVOIDANT PRESENCE	**LEARNING/EMERGING PRESENCE**	**LEADING/SOLVING PRESENCE**	**UNDENIABLE EXECUTIVE PRESENCE**
Isolated Difficult Searching for Shortcuts Pot Stirrer Focused on the Wrong Outcomes Complainer	Absorbing Watching Applying Noting Missteps Working Growing Connecting	Vessel for Answers Thought Leader Effective Unwavering Excited & Ignited Polished Actively Nurtured by Company Leadership	Loyal Room Changer Kind & Incredibly Thoughtful Natural Refuge Decisive Relentless yet Rational Relationship Capital Overflows

Note: Despite the inner work we do, sometimes organizations are simply not ready or willing to recognize marvelous talent. If you find yourself in that position, I hope you don't wait too long to make a change, because how we spend our days is how we spend our lives.
I want you to spend your life being valued.

building our high-performance team

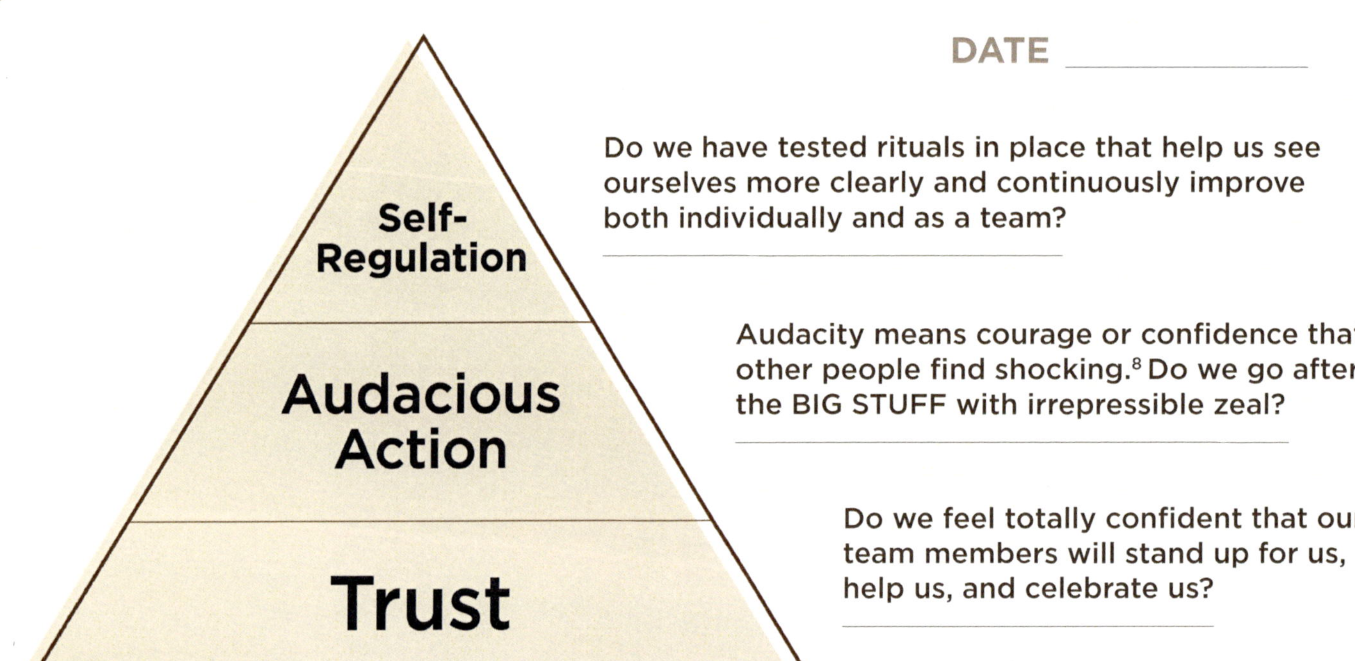

DATE ____________

Do we have tested rituals in place that help us see ourselves more clearly and continuously improve both individually and as a team?

Audacity means courage or confidence that other people find shocking.[8] Do we go after the BIG STUFF with irrepressible zeal?

Do we feel totally confident that our team members will stand up for us, help us, and celebrate us?

High-Performance Teams are built brick by brick, decision by decision. It takes intentionality, time, and focused collective efforts to build a High-Performance Team.

Based on the pyramid above, where is your team the strongest?

Where do you see the most room for improvement?

What's one action you can take today to move the needle on that element?

[8]Cambridge Dictionary

DATE ______________

7 Ways to Spot a High-Performance Team

Rooted in the idea that winning is inevitable FOR THEM. Nothing is too difficult

Rigorously untangling problems and reverently supporting ALL people

Repair is normalized, sacred and required

Real-time tension is addressed before it costs too much

Responsible with their words, taking the time to get clear, then saying it

Remarkably resilient and focused on how they—not others—can improve

Reputations are inescapable; people KNOW what it means to be on that team

What is the current reputation of your team if you **had to name it?**

____

What is your desired reputation of your team?

____

What is one thing you're willing to sacrifice to get closer to that reputation being true?

____

DATE ______________

HIGH-PERFORMANCE TEAMS REFUSE TO TRADE PEOPLE FOR PROCESS, THEY RELENTLESSLY PRACTICE CARING FOR THE WORK AND EACH OTHER SIMULTANEOUSLY.

DIANE KNOEPKE
LEAD COACH AND CONSULTANT,
PAPERWEIGHT ADVISING

Caring for the people AND the work takes time and bandwidth. What's something you're doing right now in your daily practice that you will OUTSOURCE?

deepen your connection with *your dreams*

keep our
eyes on our
own paper

DATE ___________

You are one of one and have been appointed to do miraculous things on this earth, so don't spend time fixating on the accomplishments of others!

Comparison can be deeply damaging to your psyche, process, and progress. What would your life look like if you spent less time being in awe of others, and more time thinking about your own special gifts?

What are 7 Traits you were born with that leave you in awe?

1. ___________
2. ___________
3. ___________
4. ___________
5. ___________
6. ___________
7. ___________

DATE ______________

What are 7 Reasons your life is amazing?

1. ______________
2. ______________
3. ______________
4. ______________
5. ______________
6. ______________
7. ______________

Who are 7 People who make your life better?

1. ______________
2. ______________
3. ______________
4. ______________
5. ______________
6. ______________
7. ______________

DATE ______________

If you're feeling "stuck" in your career, it's likely that you need MORE of one of these:

Which of these do you think would have the biggest impact on your career today?

DATE ______________

Career advancement is powered forward when we turn up the heat in any of these areas:

Which area are you showing up the strongest, and which could use more attention?

Brands are built one decision at a time and are always being:

- Built
- Refined
- Injured
- Rehabilitated

DATE ______

What element of your brand are you most proud of?

What element of your brand are you refining?

Consider one time you injured your brand.
What was the cause of that?

Is there an apology on your heart that would lead you down the road of repair and rehabilitation?

DATE ____________

Ensure everything you type, text, email, and post is ready for Primetime News. The ways we present ourselves in the digital space should be intentional, clear, and polished.

After all, anyone can create news based on what you say. And it's not always clear who is a reporter and who isn't. In any conversation, it can be helpful to pretend that anyone you don't know personally is a reporter.

If you need to have a delicate conversation, schedule a time and agree on the exact subject, then pick up the phone and call.

In addition to the digital space, we're also living in a world where real-life moments can be captured instantly then uploaded to the internet for the world to see. Our outward presentation and overall grooming should never be taken lightly.

DATE ____________

Let's take a moment to think about your gorgeous public image. Rate each of the places your image lives on a scale 1-5.

1 = Least polished and desperately ready for revival

5 = Most polished and enhances my reach in my sleep!

N/A = I don't use this. I touch grass instead.

Overall Grooming ____________ ____

(Clothes that represent who you truly are, neat jewelry, clean shoes, hair/nails, current dental appointments)

Website or LinkedIn ____________ ____

Instagram ____________ ____

Facebook ____________ ____

X/Threads etc. ____________ ____

healthy behavior comes from healthy people

DATE ___________

Sometimes, when humans are searching for fulfillment, we decide to add all sorts of miscellaneous things, like alternative medicines, crash diets, or expensive classes. Instead of adding to our daily routine in search of optimal health, it can be helpful to ask, "What can I take away?"

What can you remove from your life to make more space for true wellness?

DATE ______________

Keeping secrets is the highway to misery. Keeping important information in confidence is wise, but keeping secrets leads to sickness, division, and despair.

What is one way you encourage open communication in an important relationship or group, whether it's personal, a work team, or a community organization?

DATE ____________

Healthy behavior comes from healthy people. Flexibility, kindness, and forethought are not givens; they appear in people who are well.

What is the most consistent thing you do to guarantee your own wellness?

DATE ______________

Everyone wants to experience relief. Relief from their tasks, their choices, their spouses, their fears, their responsibilities.

It is not your job to consistently provide that relief for others.

What are you proud of yourself for saying no to?

DATE ______________

Being in relationship with a friend, parent, partner, or spouse without discussing individual needs is like going into a restaurant and being served whatever the kitchen feels like giving you.

This is especially daunting if you have dietary restrictions or allergies. It might work out okay, but wouldn't you rather just request what you'd like? It would probably be a lot less frustrating for all parties involved.

Just like our appetites change, our desires do too. So it's important to communicate our needs as clearly as we can, as often as we can.

In which area of your life are you just eating whatever the kitchen feels like giving you? How could you name what you want instead?

DATE ______________

Identifying a need and not communicating it is an act of self-betrayal.

What is one need you will communicate today?

Needs can be environmental, financial, social, relational, emotional, behavioral etc.

DATE ______________

**We hold our bodies in the highest esteem.
We protect them intimately, incessantly, and with meticulous planning, because that is what health requires.
We nurture our bodies no matter what.**

What are 3 ways you've loved on your body in the last 3 days?

1. ______________________________

2. ______________________________

3. ______________________________

DATE ____________

Nobody gets the glory from guilt.

What guilt are you holding onto that you can release today?

DATE ____________

Life will whisper, then it will yell.
If you can train yourself to hear the whisper and move accordingly, you will save yourself years of turmoil.

What do you believe life is whispering to you today?

DATE ____________

I was talking with a dear friend who shared her frustration about a boss who had severe and evident deficits in the following areas: self-awareness, empathy, conflict management, and team building.

Week after week, my friend felt defeated. She couldn't understand why someone so unaware, unequipped, and unwilling to change would be in such a critical leadership role.

I shared an illustration with her:

Let's pretend you need to drink a lot of milk each day. If you don't drink milk each day, you just don't feel well, and you are at risk of symptoms of calcium deficiency.

One afternoon, you realize you haven't had any milk yet so you stop at the corner store. The store has a colorful "MILK" sign in the window. When you go inside, you discover aisle after aisle after aisle is full of soda. The refrigerated shelves list the prices for milk, but there is no milk on shelves. Only soda. You drink a soda because you're parched, and you go home with a queasy tummy.

The next day, you return to that same store looking for milk. The sign is still in the window, and the cashier points you to the milk aisle, but there's no milk to be found. It's still a soda store, and you're devastated (and feeling a bit gaslit).

The next day, you think maybe the store finally got a milk delivery so you return looking for milk. No milk. Still a soda store.

DATE ______________

At some point, we must examine why we keep going to the soda store expecting milk. Yes, they said they had what you were looking for, but they have proven they don't.

Why do we return to the same people hoping they'll give us something they've consistently shown they cannot provide?

As leaders, it's up to us to take in information, see it clearly, adjust, and continue briskly on our special journey. If we give it all we've got, from a place of clarity and honesty, we can find environments and relationships that nourish us and generously supply the milk we deserve.

Where might you be searching for milk in a soda store?

Did you know that our bodies have a system called the glymphatic system that clears out waste and toxins from your brain, but this system only turns on when we SLEEP?! The glymphatic system works best during stage 3 NREM sleep which is also referred to as slow wave or deep sleep. Glymphatic system dysfunction is linked to many neurologic conditions like Alzheimer's disease, Parkinson's disease, and stroke.[9]

Sleep is an underrated advantage and non-negotiable. Sleep is required for us to move through layers of reflection and accountability. Every leader I have admired has had a clear and functional SLEEP STRATEGY.

Sleep Strategy:

Friends of Sleep - These are things you can **do throughout the day** that will help you sleep at night, such as exercise, being mindful of caffeine intake, bathing, practicing kindness, completing tasks on to-do-list, seeking support from a licensed mental health practitioner

Barrier Removal - These are things you can **do at bedtime** to ensure the best sleep possible, such as securing bedtime help with children, leaving your phone in another room, keeping a pad and pen near the bed in case you need to release any thoughts or action items as they emerge

[9]Cleveland Clinic

DATE ______________

Build Your Sleep Ritual - If you want your body to know it's time to sleep, it's helpful to go to sleep around the same time each night and **ritualize it**. Of course this isn't always possible due to travel or competing priorities, but we can make a valiant effort! Maybe your ritual could include stretching, spraying lavender pillow mist, praying, spending bonding time with a loved one, skin care, reading, journaling, or eye masks. Make it your own. Your body is full of intricate systems, and systems thrive when they are cared for consistently.

What's Your Sleep Ritual?

Bedtime: ______________

One Friend of Sleep I'll Practice: ______________

One Barrier I'll Remove: ______________

My Target Hours of Sleep Per Night: ______________

Ritual Step 1: ______________

Ritual Step 2: ______________

Ritual Step 3: ______________

the kindest person in the room wins

DATE ______________

The kindest person in the room wins.

When was the last time you recall being unkind?

What is your plan to acknowledge your behavior and repair the relationship? Repair doesn't have to be an extensive process; it just needs to be intentional.

DATE ______________

My job is to be clear and kind.

When were you clear and kind even when it was challenging to do so?

DATE ____________

We are well connected, well protected, and well respected.

When do you feel most protected?

DATE ____________

Free costs too much. For some reason, individuals and organizations got comfortable requesting talent to work/ perform for free or flimsily attaching it to the promise of "exposure."

Please allow this to be your reminder that free is expensive. The toll that work will take on your mind, body, spirit, and schedule is extensive and cannot be ignored. It makes sense to schedule select engagements or activities that align with philanthropic endeavors, but I'm talking about the sharp expert, deep in debt, who has been speaking for 20 years for free.

Overextending ourselves comes with grave consequences. We can kindly decline anything that comes our way, anytime. I bet your schedule is fully committed on that requested date and you're looking forward to staying connected! We do not give every moment of our lives to others. Doing so erases the painstaking work of our ancestors.

What is one practice you do often that you're going to stop?

DATE ____________

You are intensely beautiful.

When do you feel most beautiful?

audacity is
the accelerant

DATE

You have nothing to prove to anyone.

What have you been trying to prove?

Who have you been trying to punish?

What can you do instead that will allow you to simply enjoy the journey?

DATE ____________

It can be difficult to discern between situations where we need to "tough it out" and those where we need to leave. If an experience is negatively affecting your health—that's your cue. Do not delay. Up to 90% of all visits to primary care physicians are for stress-related complaints[10]. This is life or death.

When were you proud that you listened to your body?

[10]Occupational Health & Safety Administration

DATE ____________

Superheroes have BIG jobs!
They are tasked with saving cities and working alongside others to bring more peace to humanity!

Can you imagine what a shame it would be if superheroes, cape and all, spent their days opening bottles of water?

Opening water is an important task but it is one better suited for someone ELSE to complete, not a superhero.

YOU are a superhero! Spend your time completing tasks that align with your level of genius. Do what only you can do.

Winning is the process of making many, many wise decisions that align with your superpower.

What is the wisest decision you've ever made?

DATE ______________

The time we have to pursue our dreams while we're alive is limited, finite, and unknown. The amount of time we allow someone to waste is a direct reflection of how much we value ourselves. Partnering with other humans who understand that time is a sacred commodity helps us make the best use of our time alive.

Who is someone who is always on time and really inspires you?

DATE ______________

Time is only wasted if I refuse to learn.

What is the most profound lesson you've learned in the waiting season that will be useful when your dreams become a reality?

DATE ______________

Take the time you need to get clear. No matter how long it takes, I'm so proud of you.

What are you excited to gain more clarity on?

DATE ___________

Whatever you're building, build bit by bit and keep your eyes on your own paper. Social media has made this desperately difficult. Lucky for us, we get to manage how often we use social and how deeply we allow it to penetrate our spirits.

What's your relationship with social media?

Circle your answer below

Supremely Healthy

Helpful

Harmful

Extremely Toxic

Not Sure Yet

N/A because I don't use social media

What do you want your relationship with social media to be like?

___

___

___

DATE ___________

Some of the most unfortunate failures of audacity that I see are when people don't get something at work because they didn't ask for it. It's disheartening to me—because so much is available, yet so little is requested. Instead of asking, people start thinking about what others have gotten, analyzing the state of the world and their industry, obsessing over how the request will be received, etc.

All of the above has nothing to do with you, your time, and your talent.

All of that is noise that works against you. Instead of spending time spinning, it's much more advantageous to use your time performing at your highest level and strategizing on the timing and **words you're going to use to make your ask.**

I've seen companies give speedy yeses to talent they wanted **just because the talent asked.** A list of concessions I've granted or seen personally granted with ease:

- Mortgage Being Paid Off to Relocate
- More Compensation (In one case, a client turned down a role at $97/hour. The company called back 15 minutes later to offer $210/hour. All I could do was shake my head.

DATE ______________

Talent should not have to protect themselves like this but it's the reality we live in. To excel, we must be unequivocally clear about how we are to be compensated)

- Signing Bonus
- First Class Business Trips to Desirous Locations Plus Guests
- Going Away Party
- Taking Laptops/Ergonomic Equipment to New Role
- Elevated Titles
- Equity in the Company
- Stipends for Childcare
- Stipends for Parent Care
- Stipends for Health-Enriching Experiences

In each case above, two things were true:

1. **The talent had to be valuable to the organization**
2. **They had to ask**

What area in your career is begging you to ask for more?

DATE ______________

The Coaching Factory's Career Vitality Spectrum™

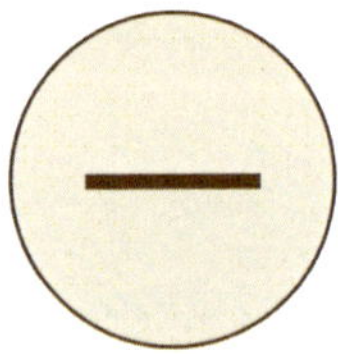

STAGNANT CAREER

- Anti-Everything
- Directionless
- No Agency In Personal Growth
- Always Looking For The Easiest Option
- Constant Liability for Team Culture

ACTIVATED CAREER

- Relationship Building
- Listening
- Learning to Speak Up For Themselves
- Seeking Guidance
- Modeling Environmental Behavior

BLOOMING CAREER

- Tapped To Speak
- Practicing Consistent Personal Care & Professional Boundaries
- Polished Media & Podium Presence
- Actively Pursuing Career Path
- Receiving Praise & Recognition

IMPACTFUL CAREER

- Taking Big Swings Undeterred by Big Risks or Innovation
- Consistently Asking For Their Needs Without Hesitation
- Masterful at Setting Boundaries & Clear Vision
- Sought After For Conflict De-Escalation Counsel
- Humble & Eager to Learn

EXEMPLARY CAREER

- Undeniable Global Reach
- Your Philosophies & Practices Are Studied & Renowned
- Highly Influential Future Builder, Learner and Teacher
- Heavily Endorsed by Universities, Brands and Organizations
- Well Connected, Well Respected, Well Protected

DATE ______________

Please rate yourself on a scale of 1-5

1=Never 2=Once 3=Sometimes 4=Frequently 5=Always

External Brand Experience

How your brand shows up in the world

I am featured in articles/podcasts so others can see my POV _____

I deliver talks/seminars or motivational experiences _____

I post on LinkedIn/social media/department sites _____

I ensure my headshots are up to date and vibrant _____

I pay special attention to how I present myself _____

Personal Progress/Asset Maintenance

How you show up for yourself

I make exercise a priority and care for my body diligently _____

I make sound decisions to honor my body with food _____

I remain up to date with doctors/dentists/estate planning _____

I keep my eyes on my own paper, not on what others are receiving or achieving _____

I don't let conflict stew; I address it _____

I spend quality time with my loved ones _____

I have identified personal goals that I am working toward _____

I have identified financial goals that I am working toward _____

I prioritize quality sleep _____

I take breaks/vacation, modeling work-life harmony _____

DATE ____________

Career Vitality

What your career choices are showing you

I receive verbal praise or awards or special recognition ____

I ask for what I want and need at work ____

I take risks ____

I receive salary increases, benefit bumps or title upgrades ____

I am rewarded with additional learning or opportunities ____

Total: ____ ÷20 = ____

1

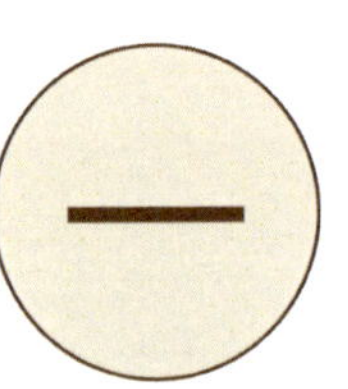

STAGNANT CAREER

2

ACTIVATED CAREER

3

BLOOMING CAREER

4

IMPACTFUL CAREER

5

EXEMPLARY CAREER

our hope is
in God alone

DATE ______________

You are an heir to the throne.
You are a child of the Most High God who owns EVERYTHING.

Where are you seeing sure signs of God's provision and abundance in your life right now?

DATE ____________

Shannon, age 50, confessed that she was working 100 hours a week for a salaried rate of $68,000 a year. When her department lost a person, she agreed to do too much, and wanted to honor her word in hopes that it led to a promotion. The people she worked with were elated because her grueling hours meant less work for them. They praised her and Shannon loved praise.

She would go home to shower, nap, then return to work. Her family was constantly begging her to stop overworking so she began to lie and say she was going to exercise classes and to visit friends. She would say whatever she needed to say to get back to work. She was literally working herself to death. If she died, the company would perhaps send flowers to her family, and they would likely fill the role again within three weeks.
There is no positive endgame for overworking ourselves.

Overworking ourselves:

- Helps people take advantage of you daily
- Signals to others that you don't value yourself highly
- Almost never leads to the promotion you're dreaming of
- Models what's okay for our children
- Exacerbates the wealth gap
- Takes your life away from you
- Deteriorates your hallowed relationships
- Enables organizational inequities

If you've accidentally agreed to too much work, raise your hand and share brilliant ideas on how the work can otherwise get accomplished. The greatest freedom is not in the conquer—but in the release.

What can you release today?

DATE ____________

Build the life you want.
Not the life you think you can get.

LET'S DREAM!
IN YOUR DREAM CASE DAY...

Who is there?

What are you wearing?

What's the first thing you do in the morning?

What do you smell?

DATE ____________

What time do you go to sleep?

How much do you sleep?

How much do you travel?

How much do you work?

Who is **not** in your dream life scenario, but is in your life right now?*

**Sometimes we grow in different directions and at different speeds. This is natural. Releasing relationships that are no longer in alignment is a quick way to change your life.*

DATE ______________

You can make one decision today that changes your entire life.

What area of your life needs the most attention?

Spend a few minutes just thinking about that area, extending ample amounts of gentleness toward yourself.

Now what's one step you can take that will propel you in the right direction?

DATE ______________

Constantly disassociating your gifts from money because you are uncomfortable talking about money leads to financial chaos. It also speedily advances the repulsive hope of so many: that you would live your life looking at everything through the horrifying lens of your own fear.

What is one action you've taken in the last five days to work toward financial freedom?

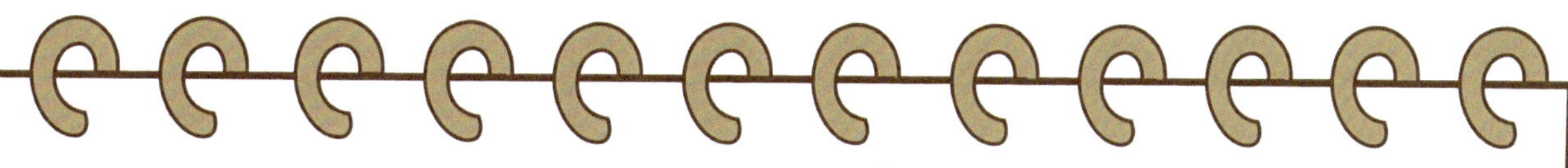

DATE ______________

No matter where you play, you should know the most about the court.

What is a topic related to your dreams that you will research more heavily?

DATE ______

What you do will be done again.
The way you do it, the world will only witness once.

What's one thing you do that no one else can do better?

DATE ____________

You don't need to figure this out, you just need to experience it.

What is something you've been trying to understand that you're just going to let BE?

DATE ____________

Many times in life, disappointment overcomes us. We KNOW we were the right person for that job, that opportunity, that promotion, or that spot on the team. Disappointment is human, normal, and a special sign that we care so deeply. It means we are alive. What I want to offer to you is this:

If that opportunity was going to bring you peace, joy, and peak fulfillment, it would have been in your path. There is something more aligned already set aside for you. The more time we spend wallowing, the less time we have to GET READY FOR THE BEST-CASE SCENARIO.

What is one action you can take today to get your body ready for your best-case scenario?

DATE ___________

It's not too late to get whatever we want. We didn't create time, so we can't control it. All we can do is surrender to the now. To this striking blue wave called life in front of us. If you ride it and don't fight it, the tide will take you to a place worth going.

What's a dream in your heart that you're going to revive today?

____

____

____

____

Who told you that you couldn't have that?

____

____

That person was hurting. They may still be hurting. I'm with you as you exhale and leave their words, their actions, their caution, and their doubt in the past. It no longer serves you, and it is not yours to hold. As we inhale, together we welcome in and expect support, kindness, encouragement, and inspiration.

DATE ______________

If you knew you only had two weeks left on the planet, what remains unfinished that absolutely devastates you?

The answer to this question offers a powerful clue about where our energy is longing to flow.

To finish what is currently unfinished, we must take calculated risks.

To win big, we must bet on ourselves.

What is one risk you can take to up the ante?

DATE ______________

Today is already designed to go in your favor.
The plan for your life was completed centuries ago, and it is GOOD.

What is the best-case scenario for your day today?

DATE ____________

In the U.S., guns kill more children and teens than any other cause including car crashes and cancer.[11]

When faced with a hypothetical expense of $400, 63% of all adults said they would have covered it exclusively using cash, savings, or a credit card paid off at the next statement. The remainder said they would have paid by borrowing or selling something or said they would not have been able to cover the expense.[12]

While many states and cities have raised their minimum wages, the Federal minimum wage ($7.25) hasn't moved in 17 years.[13]

Sometimes the job is not to get more confident or try harder. Sometimes the job is to stay alive. Life is difficult and comes with many hardships. If you find yourself in the middle of a storm, please know that:

- Every storm cloud runs out of rain
- JUST brushing your teeth, or taking a shower, or eating one meal is a MASSIVE WIN. HUGE. STAY FOR THE MIRACLE.

What is one task you did today to keep yourself alive?

[11] Johns Hopkins Bloomberg School of Public Health
[12] Federal Reserve Board
[13] U.S. Department of Labor

DATE ______________

Being ourselves is the only way to change the world. It is the best path for us.

What is a place in this world where you can fully be yourself?

What is a place in this world where you want to be yourself but have encountered resistance?

DATE ______________

You are on this planet right at this moment for a specific purpose that only you can fulfill. You have the ability to change hearts and minds. Everything you need, you already have.

What's one untapped resource in your life you will explore today?

DATE ____________

Our hope is in God alone. Life is beautiful and treacherous and complex. What we know for sure is that God has gone before us to make a way. Just because we don't know the plan doesn't mean there isn't one.

What is your favorite story from The Bible or your life that proves God's faithfulness?

DATE ______________

Integrity will take you places performance alone cannot reach. You are loved. Chosen. Called. Talented beyond comprehension.

Own the gifts that have been generously entrusted to you. May peace follow you always in all ways!

What is your biggest takeaway from this journal?

About the Author

Photography By: Mia André

Chelsea C. Hayes is the Founder & CEO of The Coaching Factory. Based in Los Angeles, she leads an innovative Corporate Training & Development firm known for designing formidable team retreats & high-energy leadership experiences centered on inclusion, leadership, & management. The Coaching Factory delights clients all over the world by delivering custom learning solutions featuring academically sourced facts, compassion, and game-based audience engagement.

Clients include powerhouse brands such as Nike, PepsiCo, General Mills, YUM! Brands, HEINEKEN, NCAA, Morgan Stanley, Eli Lilly, Spin Master (home of the Rubik's Cube), and Kendo (home of Fenty Beauty by Rihanna).

Chelsea is a Certified Senior Professional in Human Resources (SPHR), has served as the trusted advisor to 6 CEOs, and her work has been featured in The Hollywood Reporter.

Chelsea earned a master's degree in communication from Northwestern University and proudly serves on the Board of Directors of the Northwestern Alumni Association. She also holds dual bachelor's degrees in Public Health Promotion & Public Relations from Purdue University. In 2025, she was named to Purdue University Office of Fraternity, Sorority and Co-Op Life's List of 150 Most Influential Alumni in the history of the University. Chelsea served as National 2nd VP of Delta Sigma Theta Sorority, Incorporated and hails from San Jose, California. If she's not with a client you can find her being an activist, exercising, arranging flowers, traveling, napping, and being an over-involved aunt to Cadyn, Croix, and Chyla.

@ChelseaCHayes

Gratitude

Mom, Thank you for being my first example of a brilliant, generous, unbossed Black woman

Dad, Thank you for grounding me in your inexhaustible love, affection, and safety

Stately, Thank you for being my first best friend and holding me up to the light

Cheyenne, Thank you for being my perfect trifecta and reminding me of the joy available to me at all times

Hi!

I'm so glad you're here. My name is Chelsea, and I own a Corporate Training & Development Company based in Los Angeles called The Coaching Factory. I'm an Executive Coach, Team Retreat Master Architect, and Global Keynote speaker in the areas of Leadership, Management and Inclusion. I've been incredibly blessed to train audiences at powerhouse companies like Nike, PepsiCo, NCAA, HEINEKEN, General Mills, KENDO (The Home of Fenty Beauty by Rihanna), Genentech, YUM! Brands, Eli Lilly, Spin Master (The Home of the Rubik's Cube), and Morgan Stanley. I also provide 1 on 1 Executive Coaching to CEOs and Celebrities, and I love every second.

Each time I hear "Practice makes perfect," I wince because perfect does not exist! Many of us perfectionists spend our lives recklessly chasing...nothing. Life truly begins when we explore and accept ourselves wholly. Good things happen when we make space for it all—our gifts and our gut-wrenching qualities, our guilt and God's grace, our generosity and gloom.

"Practice makes peaceful!" is what we say at The Coaching Factory. The more we repeat healthy skills or behaviors, the more peaceful we feel. Peace in our decision-making and actions is the ideal destination—rather than perfection. It is my purpose to guide people to become more peaceful and profitable at work. When I've done my job correctly, my clients see positive practices seep into every piece of their lives, not just their careers.

An excellent Executive Coach doesn't give you the "right" answers.

An excellent Coach asks you the right questions, then arms you with courage to ensure you're brave enough to answer them yourself.

This journal features the most impactful content my clients have credited with helping them prosper emotionally, financially, physically, relationally, spiritually, personally, and professionally.

My prayer is that as you read and write, it sets you free. I hope you stop overextending, overexplaining and overthinking. I hope you take big swings, celebrate how absolutely earth-shaking you are, and pursue the life that you truly desire. I'd love to hear about your journey and takeaways any time #PracticeMakesPeaceful. Wherever you are in the world today, know that I am deeply honored to be in community with you, and the best is yet to come.

Always,
Chels

3 Quick Notes For You, My Special Reader:

It's important to me that you experience wellness while reading and sharing this book. All of us have an enormous variation of lived experiences that do not always elicit feelings of wellness, and that must be acknowledged. So, to travel this journey responsibly together, I asked two experts operating at the highest level in their fields to edit this work. These gentle and formidable leaders have dedicated their lives to guiding humans through growth with the utmost care.

1) This book was skillfully edited from a Clinical Perspective focusing on your mental health by Dr. Jarryn Robinson-Ellis, LMFT. Dr Robinson-Ellis specializes in the areas of trauma, mental health relapse, anxiety, depression, the unique challenges of motherhood, and attachment-related concerns.

2) This book was excellently edited from an Executive Coaching perspective by Diane Knoepke, lead coach and consultant, Paperweight Advising. Diane is also on the faculty of Northwestern University's MS in Learning and Organizational Change program, where she is an instructor on career advancement, equity and inclusion, and change management. Diane works with leaders at all levels to figure out how to get what they—and their teams—want and need. She is also my Executive Coach.

3) I encourage you to pick a page, answer the questions inside with your teammates, then listen carefully to their answers. Teammates are all around us. They are at work, in organizations we devote our time to, and certainly at home. Throughout the journal you'll see boxes that look like the one pictured to the right. If you don't feel like writing, feel free to draw a picture in the box, write something you want to remember, or leave it blank and just read! This life and this journal are designed for you to learn at your pace and in your way, as you see fit.

Okay, we're ready now! Let's begin together.

High-Octane Accountability

Actually, there is one more thing we need to cover.

This isn't a regular journal; this is designed to finally ignite action in your life. Behavior change is one of the most difficult undertakings known to human beings. It is foolish to expect humans to change alone.

We move forward in community.

Our high-octane accountability practice is used by executives all over the world, and this is a special invitation for you to try it, too!

Here's how it works:

1) Think of your accountability buddy
(This needs to be someone you trust very much and like a lot)
2) Reach out and ask them to be your accountability buddy
3) Brainstorm together on terms below
    - **Term 1 -** Decide on one action inside this book each of you would like to complete, and exactly how long you have to complete it. Common time periods are 7 days, 2 weeks or 30 days. Only you two know what's right for you. This time must be the same for both people.
    - **Term 2 -** Define the repercussions. How this works is, if Person A doesn't meet their goal within the time period decided upon above, Person B experiences a consequence. The consequence must be something that: 1) is positive for person B's health, 2) aligns with their goals, 3) is difficult but doable, and 4) has person B's enthusiastic consent.

- **Pam's Goal -** I can't see the floor in my office, so I'm going to clean it within 7 days.
- **Nick's Goal -** I will walk 1 hour uninterrupted for 4 out of the next 7 days.
- If Pam and Nick both complete their goals, EXCELLENT! Perhaps they consider setting another goal for the next week that's even more challenging!
- If Pam doesn't clean her office within 7 days, Nick will delete Instagram from his phone for 120 days.
- If Nick doesn't complete his walking goal, Pam will do 100 burpees.

Items to Note:

- Each one's success is dependent on the other person's positive progress.
- Even if things don't go as planned, the consequences are positive for their health, not negative.
- Their goals and repercussions are different because they are different people with different goals and different health considerations.
- I encourage you to consult your physician prior to agreeing to any exercise goals.

4) Both of you sign and date below

Decided Upon Time Limit for Tasks: ________________
(The same for both people)

Name: ________________________

Goal: ________________________

Consequence to be completed if Buddy Defaults:

____

____

____

Signature: ________________________

Name: ________________________

Goal: ________________________

Consequence to be completed if Buddy Defaults:

____

____

____

Signature: ________________________

This formula works because when our actions affect someone we care about, we are **careful. Care is the force behind all lasting and equitable change.**

We're really ready now! Let's get started. :)

Table of Contents